What Will Your Verse Be?

Shobha Varadhan

What Will Your Verse Be?
by Shobha Varadhan

First Impression: May 2024

ISBN: 979-889415491-6

Published by: Notion Press

Published in India

Maximum Retail Price: ₹

There's a special kind of feeling,
Whenever I think about you, dad.
The little things that mean so much now,
Your little acts that meant so much love!
There's none who could be you!

For you, Dad, a thousand times over!

This book of poetry is dedicated to my Dad,
Late Shri V. Anantha Narayanan, my friend, inspiration and guide,
who sowed and nurtured the seeds of creative writing in me.

Shobha Varadhan

Contents

Introduction

I was extremely delighted to read this exclusive collection of poems by **Ms Shobha Varadhan.**

The rhapsody of thoughts and emotions, colourfully painted in vivid word imagery is an aesthetically pleasing sensory experience.

The powerfully striking poems are inspirational, poignant and thought-provoking. While captivating readers with their literary quality, the enriching reading experience would, like the taste of good coffee, linger for long in their minds.

Wishing Ms Shobha Varadhan the very best in the success of this book, and in the continuum of her journey as a successful writer.

Mr. Ravi Subramanian
(AUTHOR)

Foreword

"Poetry is thoughts that breathe, and words that burn." *said Thomas Gray.*

I am in love with words and in awe of poets who are able to paint words of eloquence and string them beautifully, to breathe life into their poetry: once partaken, the elixir continues to refresh, rejuvenate and embellish the aesthetics of your soul, the thoughts become part of your being and the magic of the words continues to haunt you – the very experience becomes a source of *'joy forever'*, that like Wordsworth's *'Daffodils'*, makes you want to dance with them.

I challenged myself to tread the path of *Goliaths* of poetry in my tiny shoes and contribute a *'verse'* to the literary world that has always given me great pleasure as a reader. My humble verse, however insignificant, is a droplet still, in the mighty ocean of English literature.

I do believe that poetry has the quality of being *'twice blessed'* that enraptures the writer and the reader equally. Writing poetry has brought to me a great deal of happiness and fulfilment in quelling my urge for creative expression.

I do hope it will help establish an emotive connect with my readers. Even a *smidgen* of literary pleasure derived from my work would be an accomplishment I would be proud of. The book ends with a brave little *comma*, that hangs on with *hope* for many more *'verses'* to follow, God-willing!

Shobha Varadhan

Acknowledgements

Who packed my parachute?

There are always people in the backdrop of your life, silently helping you build your success brick by brick. They are the people who pack your parachute without fanfare, to prepare your path to glory.

I wish to record my deepest gratitude here, to all those who have helped me transform my passing, elusive fantasy into a tangible book. At the outset, I seek the blessings of the Almighty and the elders in my family for the success of the book.

I fervently thank **my parents** who sowed the seeds of literature, and nurtured my nascent abilities, my spouse **R.A. Venkata Varadhan** who has been my critical ally, and all my family members for believing in my abilities, and egging me on. I take great pleasure in acknowledging the contributions of **Shruthi Varadhan**, and **Laya Varadhan** who have done striking illustrations for my poems, capturing the idea behind them, and adding a visually appealing dimension to the book.

My heartfelt gratitude is due to **Mr Ravi Subramanian**, author, for penning the Introduction to my book.

I am immensely gratified **dear readers**, for your support and constant backing which has impelled me to write.

Shobha Varadhan

1. What will your verse be?

When at times, you feel low,
You have nothing to show;
Looking out of the window
Of Life, you feel lost:
As if stuck in the mid-sea,
To guide, there's no tower or tree;
No gleam of light, your spirits to lift
As you move in a directionless drift;
There's no shore in sight!
And yet friend, hold on tight,
With all your main and might
Till the tide is just right!
Give Adversity a spirited fight
And days will soon turn bright!
The haze shall clear;
The coastline will appear;
There's life to be met–
Your verse is unfinished yet!
The world awaits your part.
So hold true and fast!
And think:
What will your verse be?

PRESIDENT
SHOT DEAD

2. Carpe Diem, O Life!

Youth is reckless and rash
And vanishes in a flash.
Ere he sets out to think,
His tenure is finished in a wink!
'Carpe diem', I plead.
But Youth is too hurried!
Middle-age with many a care
Hath no time to stand and stare.
His happiness to secure
In a far-off future land,
He stretches out his hand.
And thus does he expend his span
Engaged in toils as best as he can.
'Carpe diem', is my refrain again!
But he's too busy to listen in.
Soon appears Old-age, infirm.
Short of vision, bereft of faculty,
The incapacitated Senility
Huffs and puffs, pants and rants.
But the choicest pleasures reserved
By Life to be savored at leisure
Are disused and are no more wanted.
And thus speeds by, a life wasted,
In quest of transient treasure!
'Carpe diem', I sadly murmur.
But poor Old-age, he cannot hear!

3. 'If Winter comes, can Spring be far behind?'

When the chips are down,
The ride is rough
And the going gets tough;
Danger lurks around bends;
Deterrents dent your confidence;
Challenges dare you
And you wonder what to do,
From within, you hear a feeble whisper:
Have faith, storms never last forever!
Keep going, wait for the tide to turn
The darkest night will usher in the sun!
The tiny voice of Faith brightens the day
You move on and Hope leads your way!
The night is dark, but there's many a star,
The ride is rough, but the promised land isn't far;
Move on, and don't mind the grind,
For, 'If Winter comes, can Spring be far behind?'

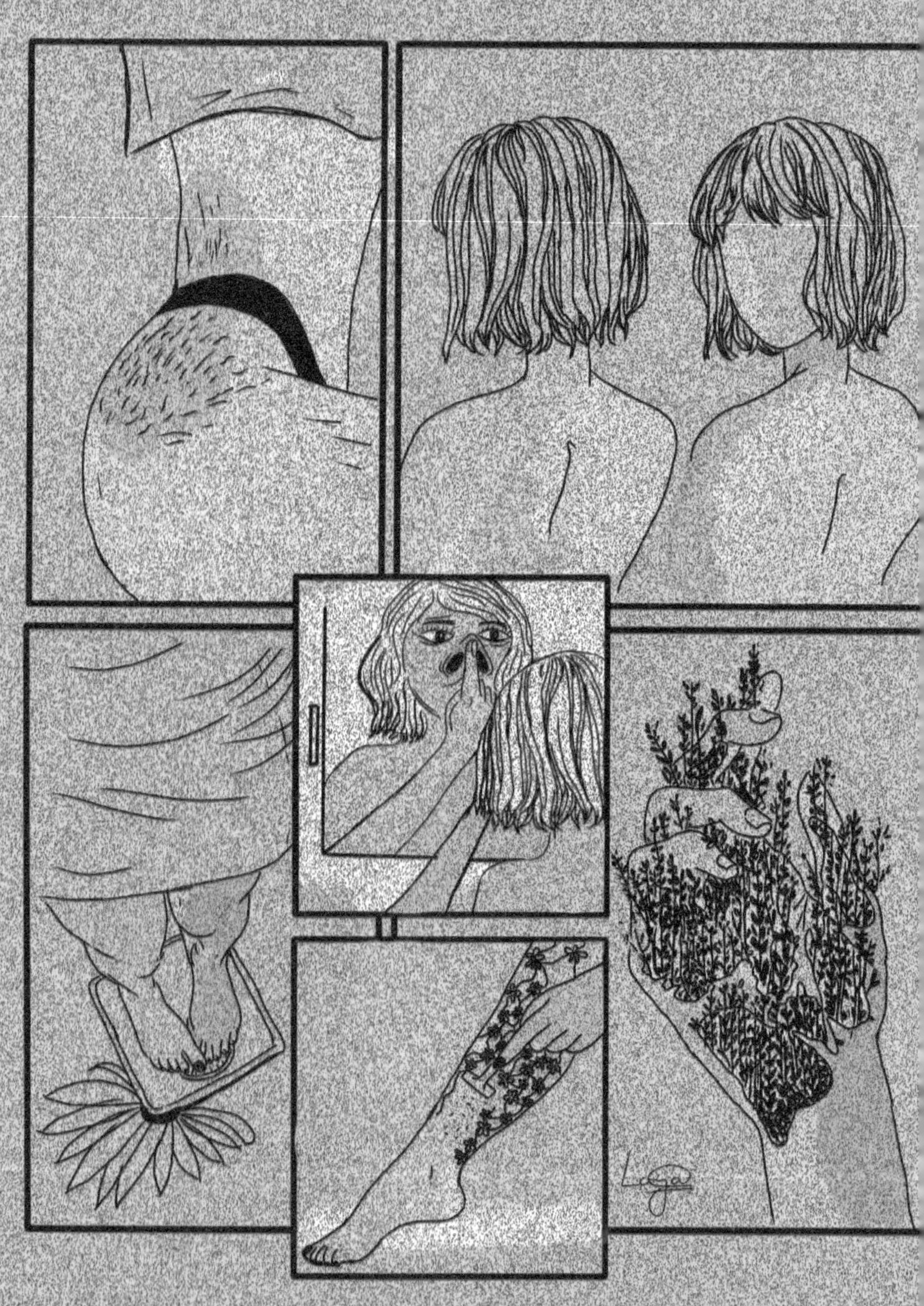

4. You are your best thing!

'Could my eyes have been rounder?',
I look into the mirror and wonder,
'My nose sharper, neck more slender,
Legs longer, build slimmer,
My voice sweeter, face pleasanter?'
Patience would've made me tolerable;
Courage, heroic; charisma adorable!
It is an undeniable fact,
That I haven't an iota of tact,
And like an oak straight and upright
I remain open and forthright!
Oh! If but benign Charm could temper;
Gentle Graciousness could garnish
And I could be a potpourri of flavors to relish!
But wait! I shan't be all that I am not.
A banyan tree cannot be coconut:
One is meant her branches to spread;
The other, to try and touch the sky!
With traits my very own, I am made.
My awkwardness was meant to be.
Indeed, I am best when I am me!

5. Wipe the slate clean!

Wipe 'em clean, oh, wipe 'em away!
Blot out the smudges;
Smoothen the edges;
Drain out the drudgery;
Dispose off the lethargy;
Clear the air of cynicism;
Cleanse away the pessimism;
Bundle out the boredom;
Sweep aside the sadness;
Shake off the sluggishness;
Free yourself of frustration;
Nod away the inaction;
Throw out the clutter;
Give your heart a flutter!
Bounce back, spring up, race
Ahead at your fastest pace!
Wipe the slate clean!
Begin afresh, start again;
Usher in novelty;
Spruce it up with your specialty;
Groom it with vitality;
Charge ahead with energy!
Refresh, rejuvenate, renew,
Discover, innovate, create anew!
Leave an indelible mark
On a fresh, clean slate!

6. Poetry of the Earth.

With picturesque landscape for her verses,
Poetry she scripts with panache;
Her expressive pen for artist's brush
She wields, stunning shades to paint –
The myriad hues, rapturous, vibrant
Depict her emotive flavors:
In sprightly rills, her youthful buoyance;
And cherubic charm of innocence
In pristine waters, sparkling ;
Her radiant smile in blooming
Flowers, like sweet maidens, do love exude;
There's promise of hope in buds unfurled;
Peace in tender grass is portrayed;
Melancholy settles on leaves in tear droplets;
The volcano, her raging ire explodes;
Gracious trees do her noble heart bear;
Her soil dons her motherly care;
The majestic hills speak of her royal pride;
The deep seas, her smug secrets hide;
She adorns with trope, her poetry:
Her bewitching beauty, for imagery
She employs; for simile, her sights scenic;
For alliteration, Nature's sounds melodic;
The rhythm of waves is her rhyme;
Poetic meters, in her cyclic clock chime;
Through the seasons, her themes manifest;
Oh! Poetry of the Earth is at matchless best!
For, the substance of her poems is 'Creation'!

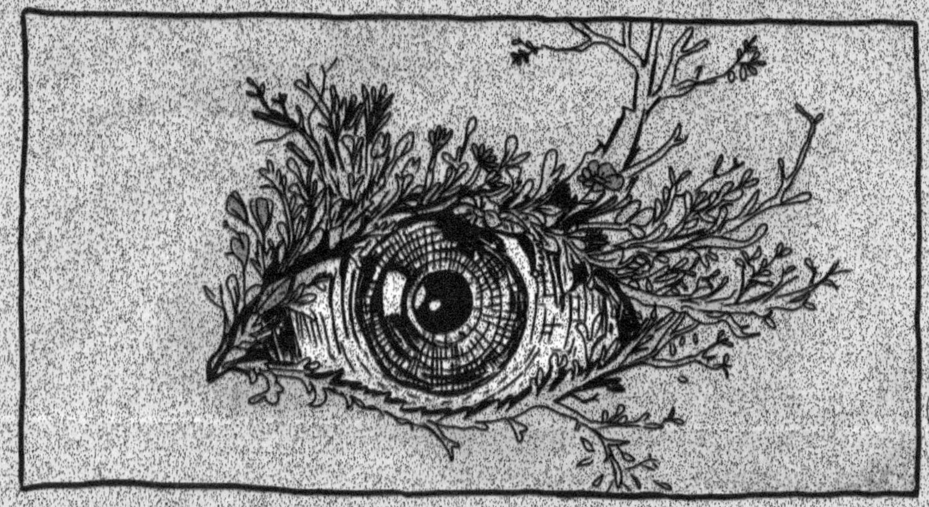

7. Taking a leaf from the Earth..

One autumn day, as I took in
The desolate beauty of the Earth:
Trees, undraped of their leafy garment,
Their skimpy arms supplicant,
Stretched upward in humble orison –
A sorry silhouette against the brilliant horizon;
Her once lush landscape, now a drab canvas;
Her vibrant colors fading into dismal hues;
I was struck with gloomy blues.
She seemed almost lifeless –
A helpless, passive witness
Of her own barrenness:
No blossom from her bosom to egress!
Was it stupor, or deep slumber?
Perhaps a meditative break
From her ever bustling oeuvre?
But I had my moment of epiphany
When in Spring, my sensual palate
Was treated to her bountiful beauty:
Underneath the lax, lethargic latency,
Were nurtured potent seeds of Creativity
To sprout forth living poetry!
So, taking a leaf, I pause with thoughtful inactivity
That I may one day burst forth with wizardry!

8. A violet, half-hidden from the eye..

A forest flower blooming
To her glorious beauty
Alas, on humanity is lost!
But whether perceived or not
She shines with brilliance,
Like a day-star of radiance.
She then withers and fades out
With quiet dignity into the oblivion.
And never questions nor wonders
What she was meant to be.
She just is, until she ceases to be!
The air, for her fragrance is sweeter,
Her happy beauty, nods its head
And adorns Nature with color;
She dances merrily to the wind,
And swishes in tuneful laughter;
She lets bees milk her for nectar,
And the butterflies caress her
With their nimble flitting feet.
She never thinks of the time
She would no longer be!
She never seeks fortune or fame
Nor claims credit to her name.
She is content to just be
And make a difference
Exuding her loveliness
Unnoticed, unperceived!
Her life, a gift received
Is returned in joy, value-added.

9. Qué Sera Sera

As dark clouds in the sky loom,
And blanket the earth with gloom,
The gold of the sunshine is stolen
Everything looks grey and bleak,
Oh! So very grey and bleak!
I mumble: Qué Sera Sera!
There's though, this single streak of light;
I hold on tight
And wait for the break just right –
Oh! A break, a break I seek!
I whisper : Qué Sera Sera!
Nature sports her infectious grin,
As the clouds weep to laugh again,
Clear light of day is seen,
And Joy takes the place of Pain!
I hum: Qué Sera Sera!
Flowers bloom, laden with nectar,
And dance and swish and swing,
And add beauty and color;
Butterflies flit and birds soar with new wings,
And hum and chirp and sing;
Bees buzz and Nature's sweet noises ring,
Resonate, resound and spring;
The grass shows her greenest green;
And Nature displays her youthful sheen;
And then I sing the old refrain
With delight, again and again:
Qué Sera Sera!

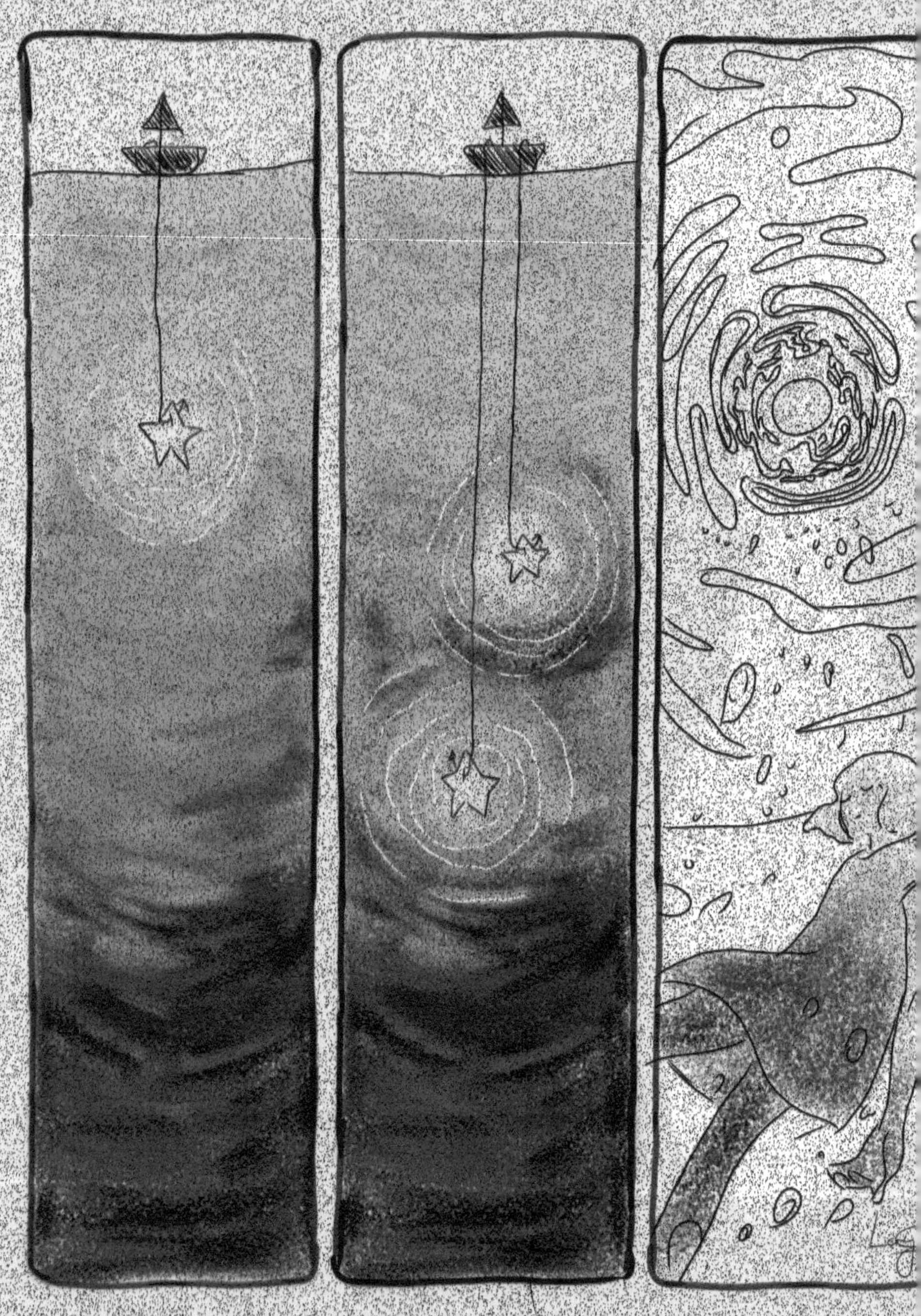

10. Paper boats that beat on..

I made a paper boat.
I set up the sail and let her float.
Down the ocean she set out,
Merrily at first, then at a steady pace.
She didn't hasten – it wasn't a race!
She kept herself proudly afloat,
Overcame the waters turbulent
And resisted the ocean current.
Bravely, she kept up the fight
Riding up many a gigantic wave.
She didn't give up or cave
In, she almost made it!
Well, she'd done her bit;
The day was spent!
And each day I send,
One more boat of my deeds
Torn out of the date sheet,
To my dream destination.
The boats with spirit, beat on
Against currents of Life,
And thus shall continue the strife,
Till the fateful date set
With ineludible Destiny is met!

11. The Wordsmith.

I am a wordsmith,
I deal in words:
Brick by brick like an architect,
I lay them together, to make perfect
Structures of thought, etched in time;
I sculpt with skilled artistry, the correct
Shape, texture, feel and expression,
So reticent thoughts find utterance –
To convey hatred, love, fear, surprise,
Sorrow, courage, anger, wonder;
Evoke pity and praise to shower;
I employ devices of poetry and epithet
To embellish language to a beauty, ethereal
Polished, refined, sublime, royal!
In my kitty are words that befit
Everyone under the Sun –
Lover, king, farmer, scientist,
The erudite, the learned pundit!
I weave magic to take readers on sojourn,
To far-off lands of fantasy and delve deep within;
I roll words on my tongue and sweeten
Them with tone and inflection,
So they sound just fine!
I am a wordsmith and design
Life out of words!

JUST
MARRIED

12. The Grammarly Wedding.

Celebrations began for the Grammar family,
When their hero, the Verb proposed
To the Adverb and she accepted readily;
The Subject, his agreement nodded;
And the Object did not object;
The Adverb was complimented
By her generous cousin, the Adjective:
Her thoughts are clear, actions wise,
Speech loving and behavior kindly;
Oh! She'd make a great partner;
"What an ideal pair!
He is action, she's a modifier",
Said the noun and pronoun in unison;
Said the admiring Sentence:
How meaningful she makes him sound,
And follows him whatever his voice!
"Oh! he's made a good choice! ",
Opined the Interjection;
For its part, felt the Conjunction,
"That's true: there are no ifs and buts";
The Preposition said: There's no doubt;
At the venue, I shall speak about
The couple in depth on their wedding day;
So blessed by everyone, they say,
The two remain happily married to this day!

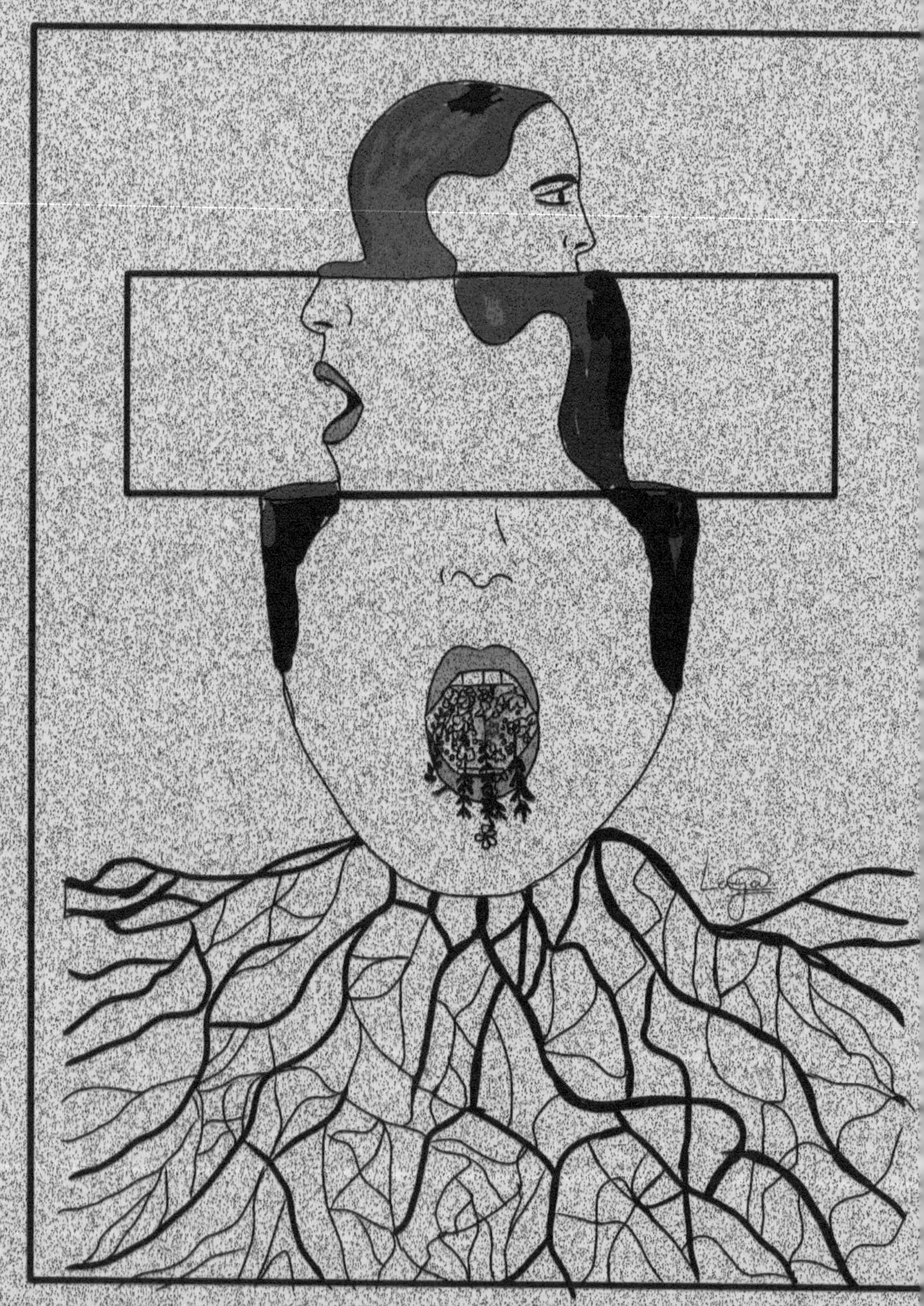

13. Words are Life!

Words blend with versatile fervour,
To depict feelings of myriad flavour;
Every shade of variegated emotion
In befitting hues finds expression;
And thoughts with their subtle
Nuances are given utterance,
The abstract take forms, tangible;
Opinions emerge with voice;
Actions find their descriptions!
Words ascribe identity to things,
Help imagination sprout wings;
With wit, they colour reason,
Brighten comprehension with clarity,
Paint with vibrancy,
The rainbow of experience;
Illuminate the intellect's nooks
With knowledge from books;
Pervade with glorious sunshine
The array of human interaction;
How words dance with abandon
To the rhythm of the lyrics of a song!
How words make Life, a poetry!
Oh! How indeed, words are Life!

14. The million lives I live!

On journeys of fantasies I embark
To lands, Utopian, remote, far-off,
Historical, fictitious, unheard of –
Lands of future, mysterious, dark,
Without Wells' Time machine!
I go around the world with Verne;
Flying with wings of imagination, I visit
Alice's wonderland, Gulliver's Lilliput;
Oh! the fascinating people I meet!
Epic heroes are never in dearth:
Hassan and Amir I cheer
A thousand times over;
I weave magic with Potter,
Play sleuth with Holmes and Poirot,
And with Mason, learn witty retort;
I relive childhood with Jem and Scout
And the Little women of Alcott;
With Atticus,parenting I learn;
Simple joys I relish in R K Narayan;
With girls of St. Clare's, I go to school;
How books make me drool!
I love Rochester with Jane Eyre,
But with Fanny, I change my lover;
I romance with Elizabeth and Darcy,
And grieve for the Great Gatsby;
I laugh, cry, rejoice, live a million
Lives with them, to forget my own!

Try drawing here!

What will **your** verse be?

Try writing one here!

15. Flavours of poetry.

Let me with the metaphoric spoon
Dole out Himalayan scoops of Irony
Into cups of Humour
And garnish it with Sarcasm,
So my point is made with Rhetoric;
May my rhyme be rendered melodic
With the lilting laughter of Alliteration,
Persistent reiteration of Repetition,
The ringing lines of Refrain
And the clang of Onomatopoeia;
Let my verses, like sweet honey,
Be tinged with the pleasing smile of Simile;
O Words! how you do ideas Personify
And address 'em with Apostrophe!
But nothing can be so worthy of praise
As the ever appreciative Hyperbole!
How I love the way Pun plays with words!
Isn't it seriously funny, Oxymoron?
Is it the end of a good beginning
Or the beginning of the end, this?
Oh! Take the call, Antithesis!
As you partake of my poetic Fantasy,
May your Cup of Elixir of Ecstasy
Be flavoured with myriad juices
Of delightful poetic devices!

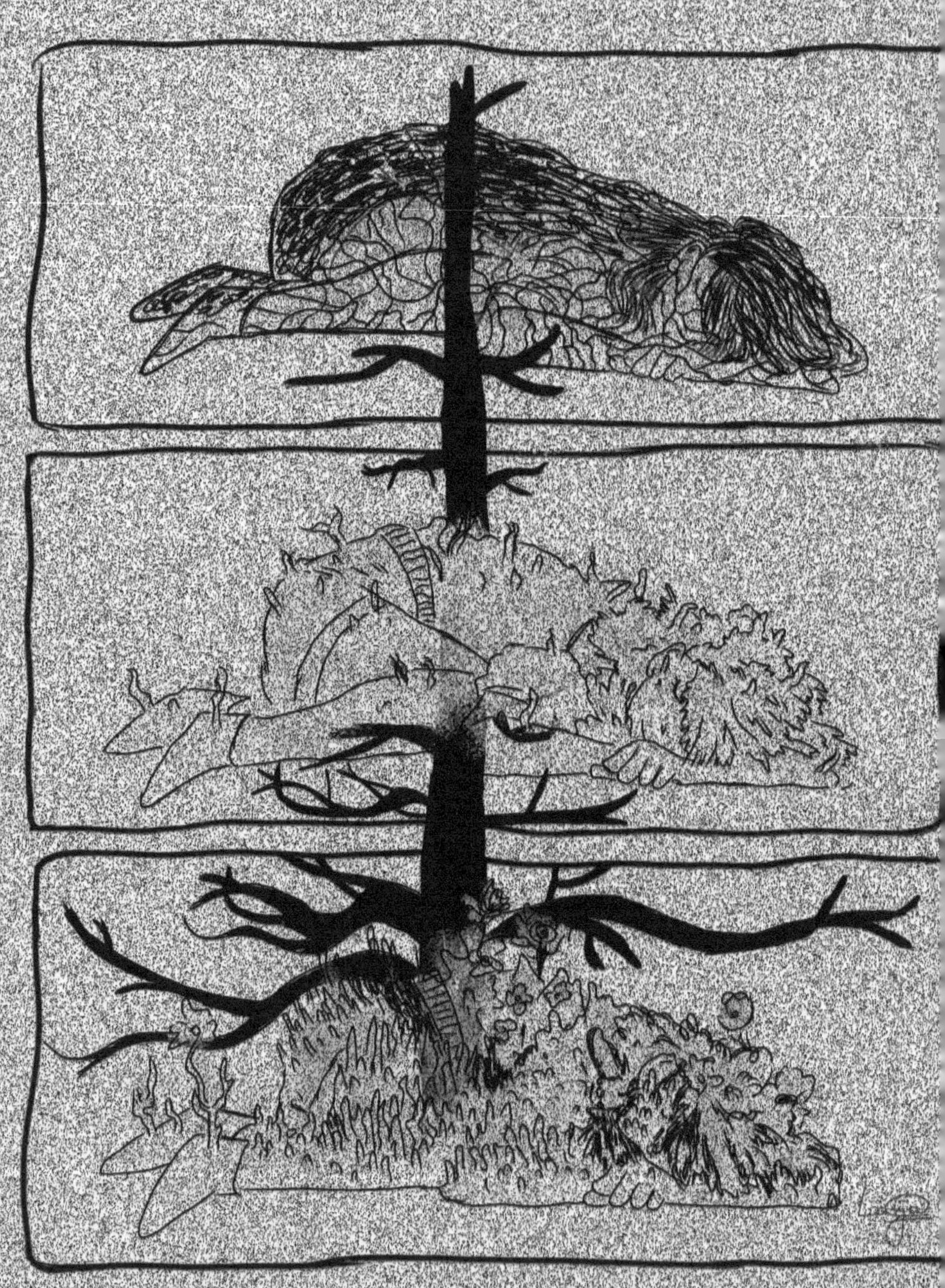

16. A dream is a seed.

It all started with a seed, tiny –
She looked fragile, tender, wee.
Her secret potent was in her, hidden.
She needed a careful nurturing regimen:
She was buried deep, ere she could sprout
And basked in sunlight day in and out;
Water from little streams she lapped
Up, and drank from the soil, her life sap!
She knew not herself, what she could do!
For days she had nothing to show;
For days we watched for a sign,
For a vague inkling, that she was fine!
But just when we thought she was done,
Buried in her tomb, before her time,
She sent out a delicate tendril hair,
A wiry antenna, to gasp for air!
She never did look back, then :
Against storms and droughts
With brave resilience, she fought!
In little spurts, she grew taller shoots,
Spread her arms and branched out roots;
Her boughs were rich with blossoms and fruit;
There stood the tree, magnificent, erect!
The uncertain time of her nascence
When examined in retrospect:
A seed, unsure and demure
Unaware of her capability
Was prodded on by her patience
And faith in herself, to create a tree!

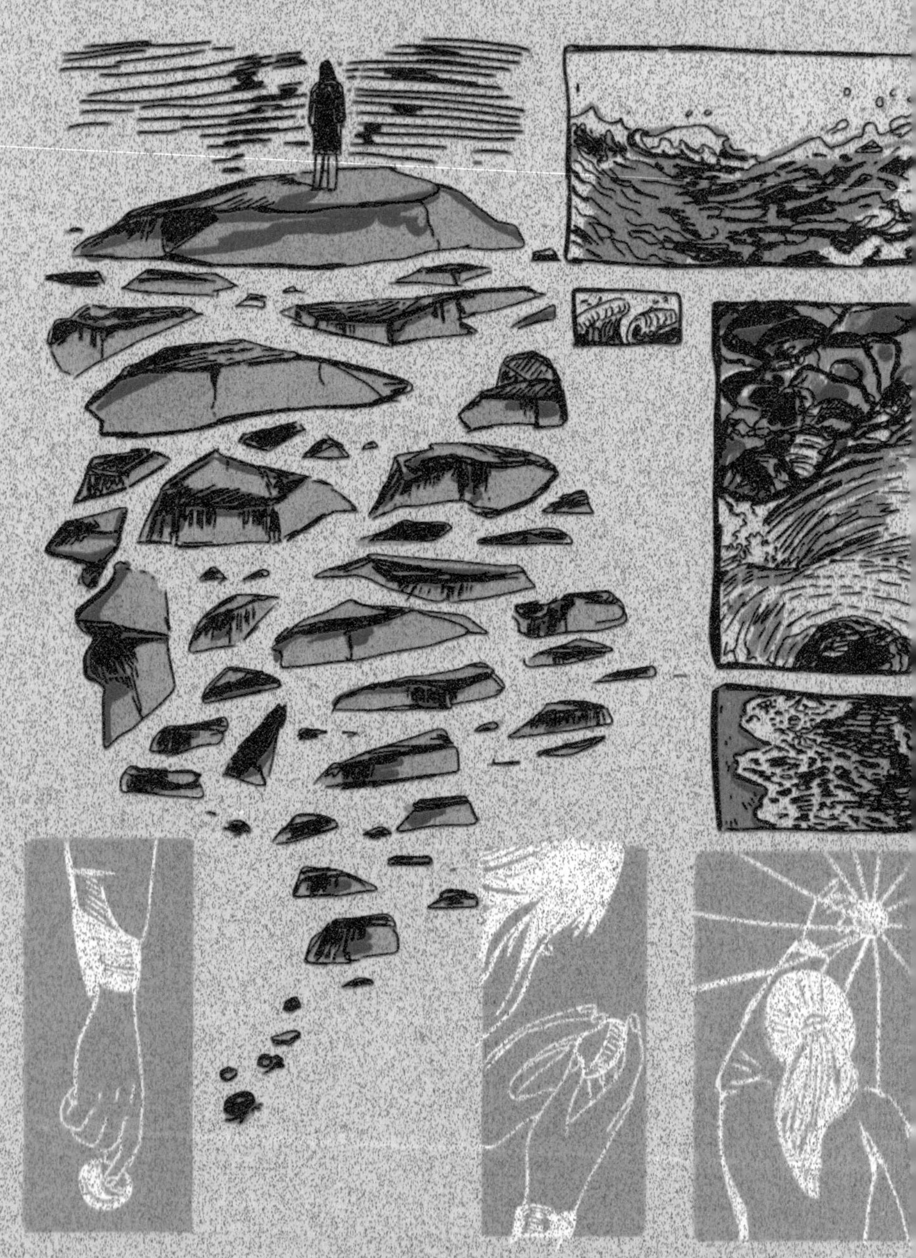

17. The round pebble.

My contour irregular and undefined
I was once crude and unrefined;
Yet, proud as proud could be,
I bragged about my singularity.
The rough river was unkind –
Tossed and turned, I lost bits of me;
Rocks and pebbles played their part
To downsize my proud heart;
As along the rocky path I tumbled,
Many an accident left me crumbled;
Ego hurt and largely hushed,
On the shingly bank I languished.
Said a baby pebble with admiration:
How round your conformation!
My smoothness in grudging tones
Was praised by misshapen stones.
In a moment of epiphany I knew
The metamorphosis I'd gone through:
Life had sliced, slashed and ground
To shape an arrogant stone, round!

18. Fingersmiths.

Deft fingers at work, making art:
Rows of rose, jasmine and marigold
White, magenta, orange, green, a perfect blend
In flowery, colourful strings of garlands;
In picturesque symmetry, dots, strokes, lines,
Pretty patterns of Rangolis and Henna on hands;
Needles through wool, weaving delightful designs;
The gardener unearthing the beauty of the land;
Marvelous craftsmanship on wood, stone and gold;
Posters, hoardings and mural art on random walls;
Dexterous fingers at work that make art:
Fingers that slice onions at the Chaat stall
And drive the nail straight into the hard wall;
Expert fingers of a surgeon;
Precise fingers of a technician;
Dancing fingers of a musician;
Adroit fingers that make fine art!
Salutes to the obscure fingersmiths!

19. None who could be you!

The tears have dried
But my heart still bleeds,
With hurt of a loss – poignant, deep,
Every time I think of you, I weep,
In silent, helpless, grief!
I think of your charisma and grace,
Of your kind, gentle love and care,
Ready wit, gems of wise advice,
Positivity, integrity and enterprise!
I think of things I miss:
The hand that held mine to guide;
The love exuded in the smile;
Pragmatic words, that my life steered!
The little things that made my day –
There's none now to look, speak and say
Things like you, or do things your way;
There's none who could be you, Dad!

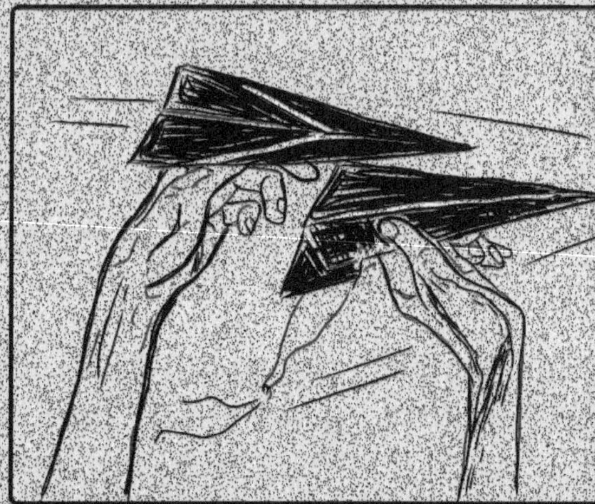

20. Those were the days!

The delightful sound of the last bell;
The hurrying feet, scurrying home;
Oh! so many stories to tell:
The inviting ground, the run around;
Mud-or-stone and Help and Chain;
The scraped knee, injection and pain;
Squabbles, cold war and pursed lips;
Fleeting enmities and transient friendships;
Childish forgiveness and the making up;
Fantasy games, paper boats, cloud-gazing;
Oh! the perfect life, of ease and lazing
The pebble-picking and pickle-licking;
Dolls, their troubles and pillow fights;
Slips between wrongs and rights;
The ant-hill, flitting butterflies and bees that hum;
Tree tops, the exploration and gathering gum;
Getting wet and the rainbow treat;
Calling out to sparrows, listening to birds' tweet;
Oh! the carefree days, the yummy food;
When life was simple and simply good!

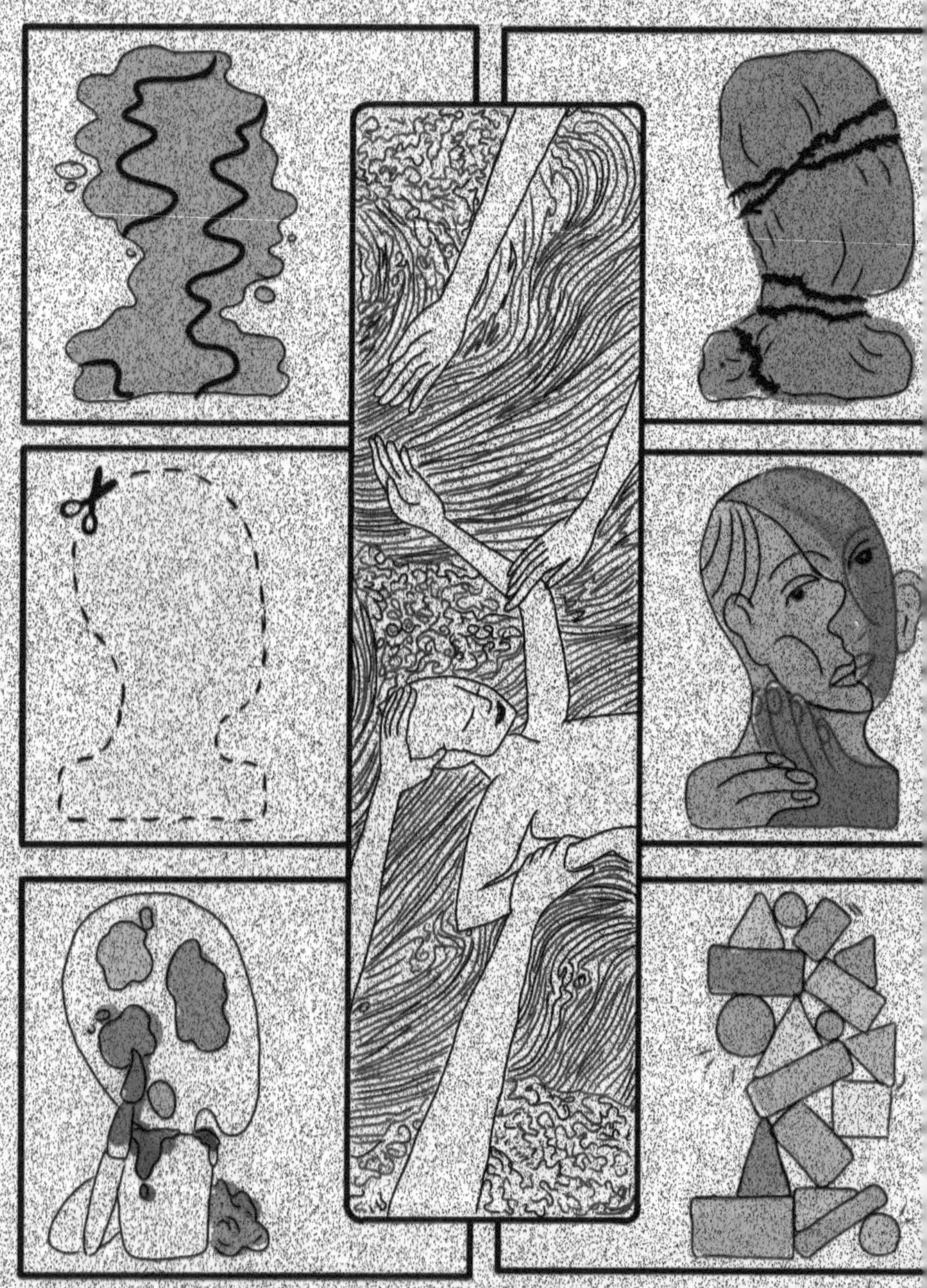

21. The Metamorphosis.

Another nondescript datesheet
Is checked off the almanac;
Life's dog-eared diary is replete
With one more insignificant
Page of tenuous incidents;
Events with promise set,
Have with natural death met;
By skeptical Cynicism doubted,
Optimism of her exuberance is deprived;
Idealism takes a back seat,
Nursing wounds of defeat
At the hands of well-armed Practicality;
Youthful Zeal has aged with weary reality;
And yet, the erosion, a painful process,
Is an essential loss
For a magical metamorphosis:
The rough ride across
Rugged terrains of life doth render
The pebble smoother and rounder!

22. Three feet from gold!

It takes just one more minute,
One step more, another feet
Of deeper dig, a little more effort,
Testing time of sixty seconds:
When you just mustn't –
Withdraw, give up hope, relent,
Yield, concede, accept defeat,
Quit, abandon, forfeit,
Stop trying, lose your calm,
Cease work, let off steam
Soften your stand, succumb
To pressure, knuckle under,
Resign, buckle or surrender!
Cling on to Patience with a smile
And traverse the extra mile
Keep alive your drive, sweat it
Out and fight with spirit!
For, at the far end awaits
Success to confer her reward!

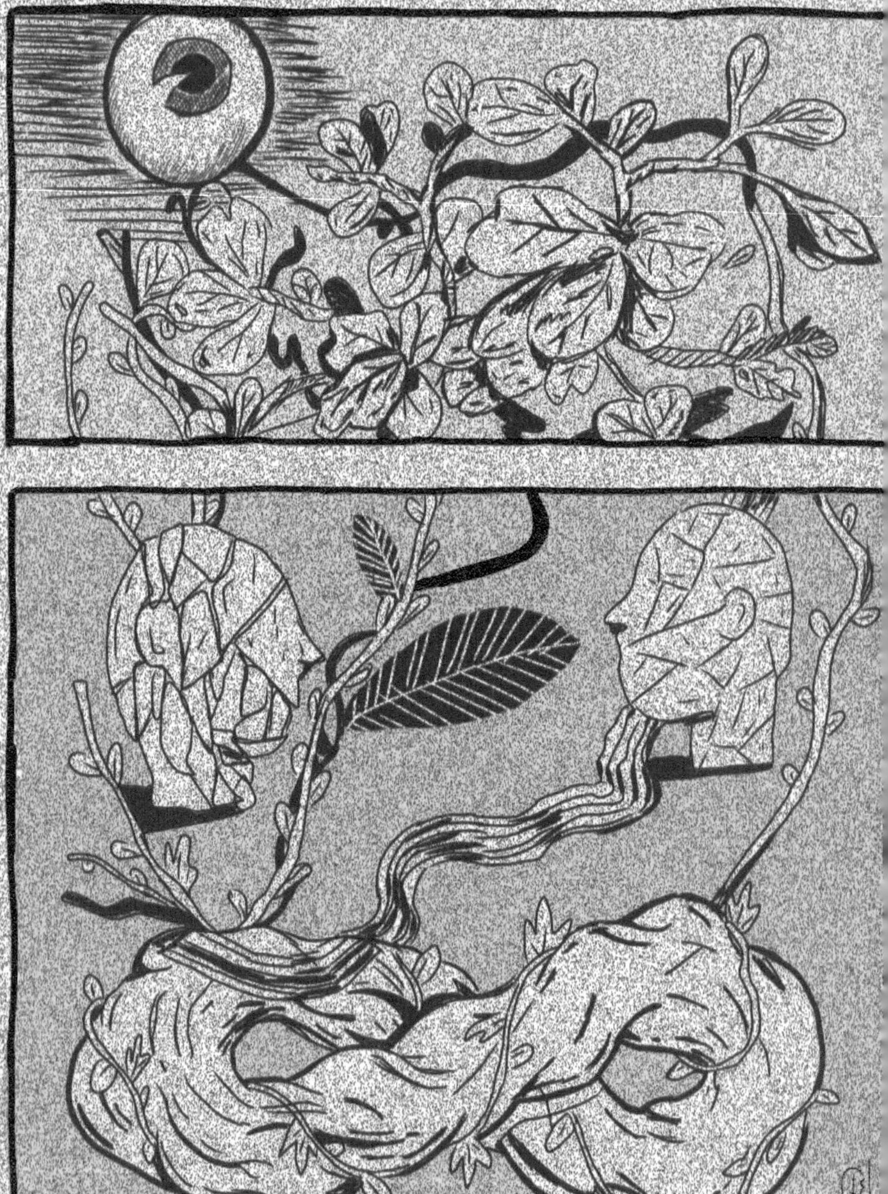

23. **Vision for my Republic.**

Let the day mark Celebrations
For our beloved Nation!
While we unfurl the tricolour,
And with pride, salute and honour
Her, let's call for resurgence
And a new India's emergence!
Our youth shall bear the torch
And dream and pledge
To lead her onward march;
Governance shall be clean and fair;
Citizens shall get their due share;
Women shall be safe
Within and outside the womb;
Corruption shall be buried
In her vile tomb;
Justice shall be reinstated
To her rightful place;
Poverty shall shed no more tears;
Peace shall be allayed of her fears;
No 'narrow domestic wall'
Of caste or creed shall divide at all;
And men and women in unison
Shall cry our beloved slogan:
"Jai Hind!", with their heads held high!

24. Lead kindly light!

My path hazy, vision blurred,
I knew not, where I was heading –
Hesitant, unsure, fumbling,
'Will I know the way?', I mused.
With faltering steps, I walked.
But with each step I strode,
A wee bit, I could see ahead –
As if by magic, the road
Cleared; Oh! Why did I fail
To see that a Hand of Might
Holds the torch of kindly light,
To lead me on my trail
Along, every step I tread?

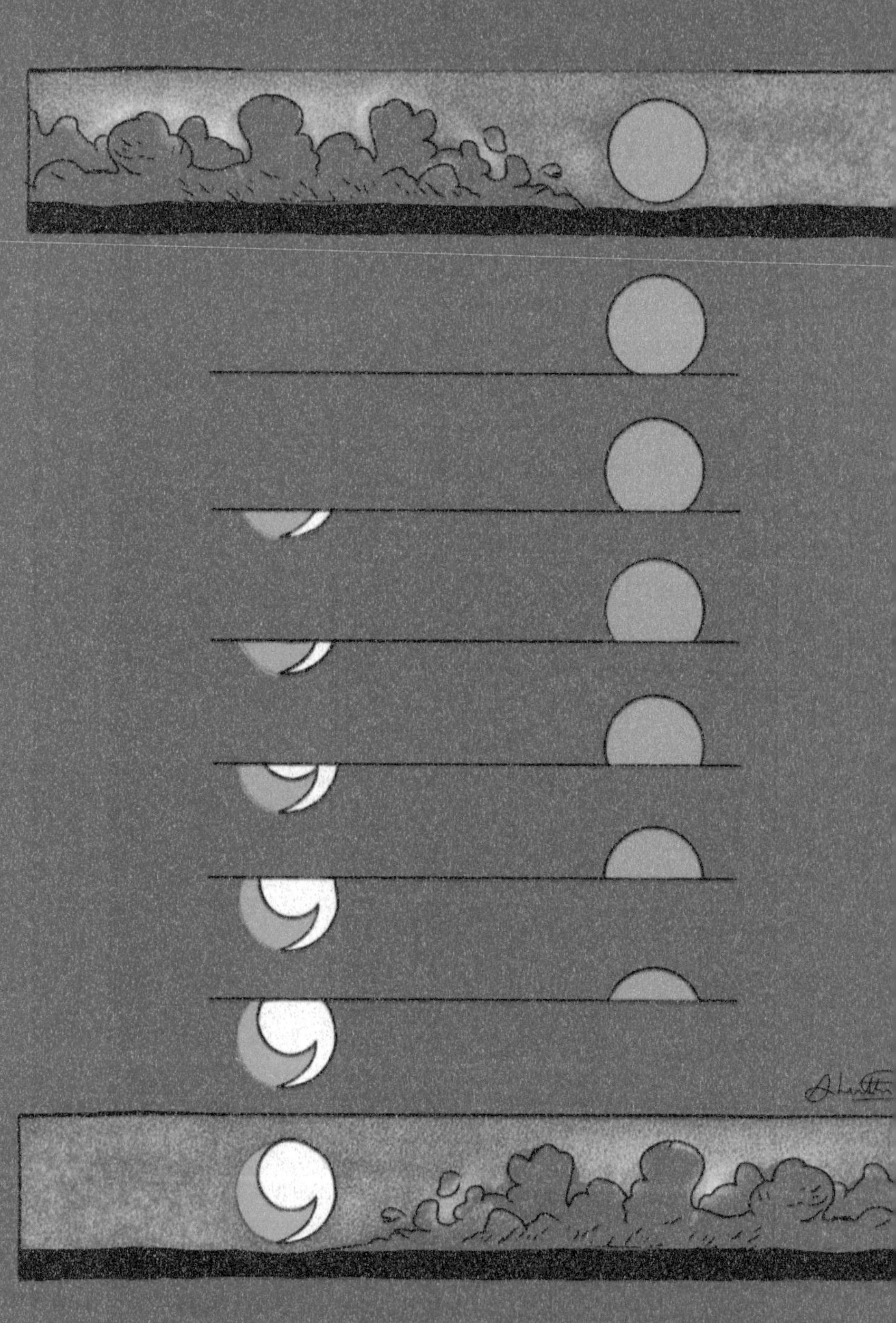

25. Hang on, there's a Comma!

The the car of Hope was brought
To an abrupt, screeching halt,
And in the deafening crash, a'most killed!
The curt Full stop was at fault.
Hope was stopped, couldn't proceed,
As if the road ahead had reached
A cul-de-sac, a sad dead end!
Opportunity her door had closed:
Oh! the rudeness left you cold!
Conversation had ceased;
Thoughts were blocked;
Possibilities lay exhausted;
The world had collapsed –
The irrevocable, inevitable finality shocked!
But Comma paused to take stock,
And Hope hoped to hang on,
Holding on to Comma's arm –
Anticipant, expectant and excited,
Of events to follow, she waited,
With suspense and bated breath:
Hope was rescued from death,
And the world rendered bright,
As the little brave Comma, upright,
Undaunted, put up a spirited fight,
Stuck it out, refused to quit
And just hung in there!

www.ingramcontent.com/pod-product-compliance
Lightning Source LLC
Chambersburg PA
CBHW021141130726
47988CB00003B/1403